# Lonely Thoughts

Dr. Kellye Bolar

Dr. Kellye Bolar

# LONELY THOUGHTS

Library of Congress Control Number: 2019901077

ISBN: 978-1-7336660-0-8

# DEDICATION

This book is dedicated to my family. I love all of you with everything in me.

# ACKNOWLEDGMENTS

So many people have helped me become the person that I am today.

Thank you so much to my mother, Jennifer Bolar, for raising me to be the independent woman that I am today. Over the years you have shown me with your actions how to keep pushing forward, even when the odds are against you.

Thank you to my grandmother, Alberta Parker, who is beautiful inside and out. Your encouraging words always come at just the right moments.

To my sister, Kelsey Bolar, thank you for being yourself and striving to exceed all expectations.

To my nieces and little cousin, Kinsley, Suri Rhae, and Arhianna, I am so thankful that God put you all into my life. You girls show so much love, and you make me want to be a better person each day. KK loves you so much!

To Dr. Gievanty Jones, thank you for encouraging and motivating me every day to continue to grow. You are the best, and I love you more and more each day.

Thank you to all my friends and family and everyone on my team for being there for me and supporting me. It means the world! I love you!

Dr. Kellye Bolar

Cover Design and Artwork: Natalie Guy

While reading this body of work, take some
time to write.
Transfer your lonely thoughts into words on
paper.

Your thoughts are precious.
Your thoughts have purpose.
Your thoughts have power.

# A Normal Day

Today

Today feels good

Regular

I haven't felt this in a while

My mind is stress free

Free of sadness

Free of worry

Free of negativity

A normal day

Today feels like I am walking

On a straight path

Room to move to the right

To the left

Front

Back

A normal day

The checklist is looking like

Rainbows and chocolate

Goodness

My heart is happy

I am smiling

A normal day

Days like today

Don't come often

When they do I am so thankful

Breathing in this feeling

The way I move through the day is

Different from those

Dark days

Those not so

Normal days

But today

Today is a good

Normal day

## That Feeling

You make me feel so good

The way you look at me when we wake up in

the morning

The way you caress my face with your hands

The way your lips press together showing a

Small grin

The way you kiss me at just the right moment

The way you take care of me

The way you motivate me

The way you look at me

The way you talk to me

The way you smell

Oh your scent

All of it

That feeling

That feeling of protection

That feeling of home

That feeling of

Just right

It's what I need

It's what I've wanted

It's here

I'm living it

I'm loving it

I'm so thankful for it

I'm thankful for you

You're the one

I love you

## Blessings

Alive

Healthy

Mobile

Job

Money

Roof

Food

Water

Family

Dance

Opportunities

Extras

Keep counting

### It's Hard

It's hard for me not to get a little upset

When I hear all this good news

From everyone

Yes

I am so thrilled and excited for everyone

Who have significant events occurring

Now

However

I am here wondering when it will be my turn

Patiently waiting

## No Clue

Unnecessary confusion

You poke and make fun of

My sensitivity

Is it funny to you

Are my feelings not important?

## **Notes**

I want you to know everything about me

Without me telling you

## Deep Breaths

Step back

Close your eyes

Breath in

Breath out

Count to ten

You're ok

Repeat

# Lonely Thoughts about LOVE

_____

_____

_____

_____

_____

_____

_____

_____

_____

_____

_____

_____

_____

_____

_____

_____

_____

_____

# LONELY THOUGHTS

## Avoided

I figured it out

I know the way to get out of the way

Out of my own way

Out of your way

No arguments

Just ended conversations

It felt good to be in control

In control of my mind

My body

My soul

My actions

My reactions

Meltdown

Avoided

## Questions

Do I love him?

Or do I just love the idea of him?

Huge difference.

# Getting Through It

Just breathe

Let it go

That's what they tell you to do

It ain't easy

Letting go doesn't even exist in my world

I get through it the best way I know how

**Get it together**

Breathe in

Step back

Look around

Process it

Take action

**Reassurance**

Desperately need it from time to time

The thought of the unknown

Makes my head feel like it's going to

Explode

Explode because of all the thoughts

Jammed into my mind

## Back to Reality

No more texting

Talking

Or meeting new men

They just forget about me after a while

Forgettable

## My Life

It isn't that bad

## Hopeful

What I know for sure is that everything

Happens

For a reason

The reason may not be clear

Right now

But soon it will come to light

God has a plan far greater than one I could

Ever imagine

## Decisions

No one can decide for you

You have to be in control of your own

Happiness

You have the power to change the way you

View life

And everything else occurring around you

You can do it

It's your choice

Decide

**It's Another Year...**

I am still single

I am still alone

This year is my year

At least

I hope it will be

# Lonely Thoughts about PAIN

_____

_____

_____

_____

_____

_____

_____

_____

_____

_____

_____

_____

_____

_____

_____

_____

_____

# LONELY THOUGHTS

_____

_____

_____

_____

_____

_____

_____

_____

_____

_____

_____

_____

_____

_____

_____

_____

_____

_____

_____

_____

_____

_____

## Nope

I can't compete with her

I can barely keep up with myself

**Bored**

Food

Wine

Empty conversations

Meaningless relations

Sleep

Eat

Repeat

# Maybe

Maybe we aren't meant to be

Maybe we are

Who's to say that this is right

Or wrong

It gets confusing

When I don't communicate completely

It gets confusing

When too much is said at once

Overwhelming

Thoughts constantly racing

And racing

Wait

Slow down

Think

Yes, give me time

I need time to think it over

Over and over again

Overthinking

Overthinking is what I'm used to

It's my norm

It allows me to play out every possible

Scenario in my head to make sure I have

Options to choose from

Options

Oh how I love options

You were once an option

One of many

Well one of two at the time

I chose you

I didn't even know you but

I chose you

It was something about you

That drew me in

That made me choose you

Instead of that other one

One

You're the one

My one

I don't want another

One

One is all I need

Complicated is not what I do

It's not my norm

Or is it

No

I need simple

Basic

Regular

You're anything but regular

That's what I know

But it's not what I want or need

Advanced

Top of the line

All the way up there

That's you

That's me

Maybe that's why I think we are meant to be

Maybe

**Support**

I want to be there for you

In every way possible

Allow me to hold you up

Like the walls of a house

I'm here

I'm not going anywhere

Lean on me

I got you

Let me help you stand

## Doubt

I don't know how to structure

A sentence to make sense

For my own understanding

How do I open up to you

When I don't even know the words to say

There are so many things

That have to be thought about

Before my thoughts are even given

Life in your world

I'll keep them to myself for now

At least until I'm sure

There's the doubt

## He Doesn't Suck...

I'm still learning him

Patience is important

I'm still learning

Slow and steady

Slow

Steady

Dr. Kellye Bolar

## Snap Back to Reality

It's all a game

In his eyes

And you are just

A pawn

# Lonely Thoughts about GROWTH

_____

_____

_____

_____

_____

_____

_____

_____

_____

_____

_____

_____

_____

_____

_____

_____

_____

# LONELY THOUGHTS

_____

_____

_____

_____

_____

_____

_____

_____

_____

_____

_____

_____

_____

_____

_____

_____

_____

_____

_____

_____

_____

## Nothing

Nothing is as it seems

Ever

It's all a fantasy

Movement is weakened by the

Negativity from those that surround me

Nothingness

Takes over me with every bad thought

Thrown my way like a dart to its target

I feel like nothing

Is going my way

Nothing

**Expectations**

Expect nothing

From everyone

When you do

You will always

Always

Be surprised

When they exceed your

Expectations

# Bright

I want to be a colorful rainbow

In someone's cloud

His cloud

Blue or gray

**Healing**

What does it mean to be completely healed

Is it when you're happy

When everything is working as you want it to

Is it when you smile nonstop

Is it when everything works just the way you

Dreamed it would

Healing is a process that is not the same for

All

My healing occurred when I categorized my

Thoughts into folders in my mind

Happy

Sad

Work

Family

Relationships

Healing looks different on everyone

The process isn't

One size fits all

## Little Things

It's the little things that make me happy

So why am I still here

When you don't do the little things

**Words**

Your words

Hold so much weight

Making me feel like I'm trapped

I hold on to the things you say

Like it's the life of me

And letting them go would kill me

Your words

## Sight

Completely blinded

By the thought of you

I tried to make my fantasy

A reality

## Today

Today

I feel good

I feel loved

I feel secure

Today

# Needs...

Love

Attention

Time

Communication

## Words

Your words run off your tongue

Like water from a hose on a hot summer day

I want to catch every drop with my mouth

I want to taste every drop on my tongue

I want to feel the vibration of your words

hitting my soul

I want to hear every breath you breathe into

those words

I want to smell the scent of your words in

every memory

I want to see your lips reveal the words of

your heart

Your words

# Lonely Thoughts about HEARTACHE

_____

_____

_____

_____

_____

_____

_____

_____

_____

_____

_____

_____

_____

_____

_____

_____

_____

_____

# LONELY THOUGHTS

**Up and Down**

My emotions about you

About the feeling I get when you are near

My emotions about you

About the feeling I get when you are away

Up and down

Like a child getting excited for a special day

Up and down

Like a rhythm of that perfect song

Perfection

Does it exist

In my world it's what I strive for

When it isn't reached

Up and down I go

Trying to make the best of it by

Perfecting every part

Every part dissected before I

Spit the words out to you

Up and down

Back and forth

In my mind

Should I release my heart to you

Should I allow you in

Up and down

Indecisiveness surrounds me

Up and down

## Love Me

Love me more than I love you

Is that possible

If it is then it's more love than I could

Ever imagine

It's insane to think that someone could

Love me

So much

It's insane to think that I could love someone

So much

## This Feeling

The feeling of uncertainty

It's driving me crazy

Thoughts about us

Running through my head

Causing me to think about the pain

The pain that my heart feels when we aren't

Right

When we aren't right in my head

It's driving me crazy

The constant thought of

What if

What could be

What will be

Back and forth goes my mind

Wondering about the status

Dead

Alive

It's driving me crazy

Crazy

## Get Out

I gotta get out

Out of this pattern

The same ole thing

Every

Single

Day

**Pain**

Sadness and headaches

The pressure of my thoughts

Against my head creates

Stress

How do I release it?

How do I make it go away?

Pain

I am the cause

I am the treatment

Getting myself to understand that

I am in complete control

Control of my emotions which cause me

Pain

Control of the sadness that comes and goes

Like

Night and day

Pain

I can get through it

I believe it

# Lonely Thoughts about SELF-ESTEEM

_____

_____

_____

_____

_____

_____

_____

_____

_____

_____

_____

_____

_____

_____

_____

_____

_____

# LONELY THOUGHTS

**This Ain't It**

This life I'm living

This ain't it

Going through the motions

Each day

Like a clock

Ticking

Timelessly

On a wall

This life I'm

Living

This ain't it

Broken

Smiles

Trying to fix themselves to say

I love everything about my life

Well

This life I'm living

This ain't it

**Untitled**

Conversations

Discussions

Talks

Are we resolving anything

Are we getting to the bottom of it

## Little Black Girl

You

You are my inspiration

The words you use to form sentences and

thoughts

Make me wish my mind wasn't so exposed to

the world I live in

I want to be in your world

Little black girl

Your world is filled with greatness

Little black girl

Your world exudes happiness

Little black girl

Your innocence allows you so many

opportunities

Little black girl

You can be anything you want to be

Little black girl

Don't ever allow this world to pull you away

from dreaming

Little black girl

You are worth every good thing there is

Little black girl

You make me proud

Little black girl

You are enough

Little black girl

You are a star

Little black girl

You are a queen

Move as such

Little black girl

You have all the power

## Who You Are

I love everything about you

Don't ever change who you are

That's what I tell you

Really what I'm saying is that

I love most things about you

Don't change those things

I love that you tell me you love me

I don't love the way you only show me you

love me on your time

I love that you hold me and kiss me

I don't love that you only hold and kiss me

when it's convenient for you

I love the talks we have

I don't love that our talks sometimes lead to

arguments about stupid shit

I love the way you make me feel

I don't love the way you make me feel when

you are upset

**How to Lose a Guy...**

Be yourself

Be sweet

Text him

Call him

Have a job

Work hard

Do too much

## Laughter

I just think it's funny how…

For most people this is the

Prelude to every argument

The bridge to every assumption

The filler to every thought

But for me

I really do think it's funny

If I say it's funny

## Lonely

One morning I woke up

Feeling like I could conquer the world

All was right with me and

My life

It was great

But in a split second

Due to an action made by

Someone else

My heart felt

Lonely

As I sank into myself

I gasped for air

I couldn't breathe

I couldn't think

I couldn't even fucking talk

It was as if someone had stuffed me with

cotton like a teddy bear

And stitched my mouth closed

Lonely

I just felt

Lonely

Left in the dark

In an empty room

All by myself

Within myself

Fighting myself

Lonely

The exit was impossible to find

It was covered by

Every negative thought that had entered my

mind

All the ways things could just

Crumble

Lonely

But you were right there

Next to me

Beside me

With me

Yet we were so far apart

On two different planets

In our own worlds

Lonely

# Lonely Thoughts about PATIENCE

# LONELY THOUGHTS

## Mental

Never allow a person, a feeling, an idea, or
even a thought to determine your mental state
Keep fighting through to sanity until you
reach your highest point

## Planting the Seeds

I like it when you wear your clothes more

Fitted

I changed my wardrobe

I like the way your face looks without makeup

I transformed to a more natural look

I like it when your hair is braided

I kept it braided

I like it when you think like me

I explored his way of thinking

I like it when you move like me

I mimicked his every move

I like it when

I like it when

I like it when

I like it when I am me

I am me

# Better

Today

I am a better me

Than the me I was yesterday

I am a better me

Than the me I was last week

I am a better me

Than the me I was last month

I am a better me

Than the me I was last year

## Smile

Through all of the pain and the heartache

I still remember your

Smile

The brightness made every room light up

So vibrant

So loud

So much joy

Behind that smile there are lies

Deception

Damage

And so much pain

The hurt that I hurt when I think about that

Smile

Is almost as much as the exhilaration I feel

When I think about that

Smile

It's all the same behind that

Smile

There are beautiful memories

Memories of our past

Memories of our shattered dreams

It's all behind us now

Behind that

Smile

## Better

It is always a good feeling

Reaching further and further into my potential

Discovering my true power

Has altered my perception

In a good way

I see the good in things I once thought

Could never be

Better

I see it

I see me

I am better

## The Wait

Tick tock goes the clock

Isn't that how the old saying goes

Watching the hands tick

Each second passing by

Slowly

Why must I put myself through this misery

This pain that I have caused myself

## Expectations

Expect nothing

You will be happier that way

## The Talks

Questions running through my mind

Did I do something wrong

Are we ending

Did I say too much

Did I not say enough

What did I do

Wait

Redirect

What did he do

Did he say too much

Did he not say enough

## Questions

Is it just a bad day?

Or am I really over it?

# Lonely Thoughts about HAPPINESS

_____

_____

_____

_____

_____

_____

_____

_____

_____

_____

_____

_____

_____

_____

_____

_____

_____

_____

# LONELY THOUGHTS

_____

_____

_____

_____

_____

_____

_____

_____

_____

_____

_____

_____

_____

_____

_____

_____

_____

_____

_____

## Love

It's like a rollercoaster

The ride looks so appealing from afar

Scary, but still delightful

The thrill of knowing how much excitement

will come from

Riding makes my heart beat extremely fast

Holding on to that feeling is what is

frightening

Will the sensation remain

Will it dwindle away

Walking up to love

Looking love in the face

And taking in every bit of it that it has to offer

That is the kind of good love I crave for

I want to ride that ride

Each and every day

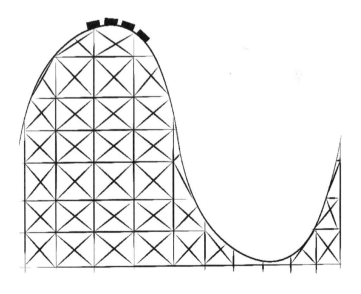

**The Way**

Show me the way to your heart

The journey is tough

I need to know every path

Please will you show me

The way you move with such zeal

Excites everything inside of my

Desperate body

I need you to show me the way

Show me the way to our happy place

Lead me like a conductor of a symphony

Gracefully I will follow

Show me the way to your heart

**Frustrated**

You denied me

To help get me motivated

I love you

But I am frustrated

At times your tactics are bizarre

In the moment my love goggles are so thick

I can't see how serious you are

You use separation

And frustration

To get me motivated

I can't stand you right now

But I'll appreciate it

This will soon all come to an end

The thought and space I'm in

Frustrated

## Your Ways

The other day I was thinking about how lucky

I am

The other day I was also thinking

About how angry I get

Angry because of the "weird" space we enter

Frustrated by the mix ups in communication

It never fully makes sense

When we are having our conversations

It's not until hours later that I finally

Realize what you meant by the

Words you chose

Patience

Your ways are, at times, unorthodox

My mind has not been to many of the

Areas you take me

The virtual field trips through your

Thoughts have been what have

Kept me

Around

Well, that among other things
Your ways allow me to feel
Every emotion at different levels
At different times
Continue to show me
Your ways

# The Day

Stomach in knots

Waiting for the confirmation text

Smiling and laughing with my friends

Nerves at an all time high

Thoughts racing

Nothing to wear

Buy a new shirt

Relax a little

Wait patiently

Sip some vodka

Breathe

Driving with butterflies

Call mom

Text friends

Pull up at restaurant

Wait and pray in car

Contemplate turning around

Snap out of it

Exit the car

Walk into the restaurant slowly

Smile on my face

There he is

Eye contact

Hug

Strong

Sigh of relief

Introductions

Smiles

Sushi

Laughs

Connections

Chemistry

Check please

Exit the restaurant

Car

Conversation

Goodbyes

Eye contact

Chin up

Kiss

An electric kiss

Soft lips

Butterflies

Heart racing

Sigh of relief

Future thoughts

That was the best day

**That's What They Say**

The answers to your problems can be found
within

That's what they told me

If you are feeling down just pray about it

I did

That's all I did

Without action

Prayer doesn't work

I couldn't just sit back and wait for all the
good things to come to me

I needed to do something about it

Sit back and wait

That's what they say

No

I won't sit back and wait

I won't let the good things just appear

My prayer and actions will lead me in the right
direction

That's what I say

# Lonely Thoughts about STRENGTH

_____

_____

_____

_____

_____

_____

_____

_____

_____

_____

_____

_____

_____

_____

_____

_____

_____

_____

# LONELY THOUGHTS

_____

_____

_____

_____

_____

_____

_____

_____

_____

_____

_____

_____

_____

_____

_____

_____

_____

_____

_____

_____

## Mask

Some things are better when they remain
hidden
Revealing my true self to people
Who care for me is one of the most difficult
things to do
When I come to the light
I am fully exposed
Facing all that comes my way
Revealing myself
Stepping from behind the mask
The mask that protected me when I was
scared
The mask that allowed me to showcase all of
me
To the world
I am taking the mask
Off

Dr. Kellye Bolar

## Reassurance

Call me your baby and tell me you love me.

**Affirmations**

You are so beautiful.

Today is the day that you make a change, no matter how big or small.

You are worth so much more than you know.

Continue being your best self.

You are enough.

I believe in you.

I love you.

**Notes to Self**

Lord, give me the strength.

Don't take things personal.

Think of others.

Be clear and specific of needs.

Let it all out.  You'll feel better.

## Mind

Only open two files at a time.

## Encouraging Note

I hope today is a little sweeter.

**I am the Cause**

I am destroying my own life

With the thoughts bottled in

I am destroying my own happiness

With the frequent confrontations

I am destroying myself

With destroying myself

So much pressure is being put on my back

Each day a new load is added

Not because of someone else's doing

Because of my own

I am my heaviest weight

I am my worst nightmare

I am the cause

**Do You**

Walk like you talk

Practice what you preach

Use what you know

Do what you've learned

**Protection**

Every month I wonder

If I made a bad decision

Protecting myself from all things

I find negative is a norm for me

Unwanted people and situations

don't usually hang around me at all

# Lonely Thoughts about CHOICES

## Future

I want to bring life into the world

Surrounded by silence, loved ones and my

favorite candles

## Numb

Flash back to that summer

The summer of no remembrance

Memory lost to the high dosage

Why was I sad again

How did I get here

Numb to all pain

Numb to all feelings

Numb to every emotion

Summertime sadness

Played as the soundtrack to my

Numbness

**What If...**

What if I didn't hold back

What if I tell them how I really feel

What if I told the guy who I used to love how

much I actually thought of him

Could my words have had that much power

What if

What if I didn't hold back

What if I tell them how I really feel

What if I had told him to stop

Would he have listened

Could my words have had that much power

What if

What if I didn't hold back

What if

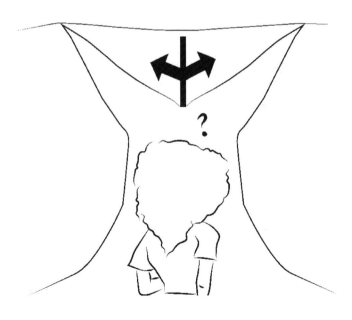

**Rejection**

Thoughts enter my head

As you open your mouth to speak

What will you say?

How will I feel?

Then you say you're leaving

And there I am

    Standing

        Alone

            With a feeling of being rejected

**Forgiveness**

Forgetting what you did to me

Will never happen

Forgiving you for making me feel

Weird or low

Is something I have to deal with

# Jealous

It's a word that burns

Burns when I hear it as if it describes me

I'm not usually the jealous type

But when I'm pushed to a certain level

I can be evil

Pure evil

Words roll off my tongue

Like water in a downward stream

Like a massive wave in the ocean

# Liar

Your deceitful words hurt me

You lie your way to success

You play the game so well

You are the best liar I have ever known

Teach me the way

You lie

I want to play your game

I want to play by your rules

I want to be a liar too

## Eyes

I'm so in love with you

Your eyes hypnotize me each and every time

You look at me

Don't stop looking at me with those eyes

## Stuck

I am stuck in a place that is

Toxic for my health

I choose to stay because it is easy

It is what I know

It is what I am most comfortable with

I don't want to be stuck anymore

I want to break free and run to my true self

I don't want to be stuck anymore

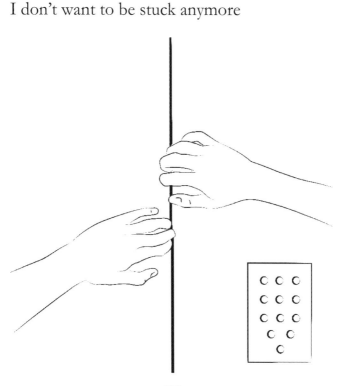

**Fatherless Child**

What is a father?

What is his purpose?

Am I supposed to have one?

Thoughts flow through my mind about my

Family parts

That were

Missing

Did I really miss that much?

Fatherless is all I knew

# Lonely Thoughts about HEALING

_____

_____

_____

_____

_____

_____

_____

_____

_____

_____

_____

_____

_____

_____

_____

_____

_____

## Silence

It's a game you play

When you want your space

I don't like the quiet game

## Hide and Seek

If I hide

Will you seek me?

Will you come after me

And save me from myself?

The comfort of knowing

That you will be right behind me

As I run and hide

Is worth gold

I need you to want to find me

I need you to want to protect me

I need you to want to hold me

I need you to want to love me

I need you to want me

I need you

Seek me

**Let It Be**

What will be

Will be

Be patient

And do your part

You can only control

Your actions

**Focus**

When I question whether this will work

Or not

I always wonder what you are thinking

Are you thinking of me?

Am I even a small factor in your equation?

No

Your focus is on other things

You have deemed more important

Than I will ever be to you

Your focus is on yourself

You are so selfish

I fell in love with a selfish man

How?

How could a woman like me

So needy

Fall for a man who only thinks of

Himself when he looks into the future?

Your focus isn't on elevating OUR lives

It's all about YOUR life

I'm nowhere in your equation to solving life

You plus me does not make sense

In your world

You are your focus

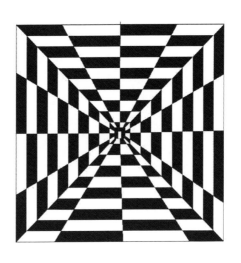

## Lonely Thoughts

Sometimes

All you need

Is time to breathe

Sometimes

All you need

Is a little music

And your

Lonely thoughts

## Growth

Relationships that used to exist

Don't exist anymore

Lost conversations

Mixed emotions

We grew apart

Maybe one day we will find our way

Back

Back to how it used to be

Maybe

We grew apart

We have gone our separate ways

Growth

**Memory**

I didn't always feel

Welcome in my own world

The public display of my emotions

Sent me over the edge

Suddenly quenching for wetness

On my tongue to allow me to

Speak

Words poured out of my mouth

Rapidly

Sounding like quiet murmurs from a distance

There was no room for cheers for myself

I never felt like I deserved the

Recognition or to be

Noticed.

Dr. Kellye Bolar

**Secret**

Setting the scene had to be a breeze

Invite them into your home

Offer them the beauty and luxuries they

Seek

Relate to their needs so they will

Accept you

Offer a new way, idea, or thought

Make it about them

Sift through the ones who are loud enough to

not hold it in

Seep your hands into the most vulnerable prey

Take advantage of the entire situation

As if the physical, mental, and emotional

discomfort won't exist

Wipe your slate clean of all unwanted residue

Bring it back to normal

Shhhh.....

Keep the secret

## Goodness

There is so much goodness going on in the
world. We get so caught up in all the
negativity that we forget all the positive things
happening in our lives and in the world
around us. People are having babies, getting
married, telling someone they love them for
the very first time, getting a job promotion,
losing that extra weight, gaining extra weight,
learning to walk, learning to talk, learning to
read, going to bed in a house they call home,
taking a clean shower, drinking clean water,
eating food, finding love, finding God,
discovering who they truly are, and so much
more. Focus on the positive happenings
more, and it will all come back to you.

## The End

It's the end

Again

# Lonely Thoughts about YOU

_____

_____

_____

_____

_____

_____

_____

_____

_____

_____

_____

_____

_____

_____

_____

_____

_____

_____

_____

_____

_____

_____

_____

_____

_____

_____

_____

_____

_____

_____

_____

_____

_____

_____

_____

_____

_____

# Just Keep Writing

_____

_____

_____

_____

_____

_____

_____

_____

_____

_____

_____

_____

_____

_____

_____

_____

_____

# Writing is Therapy

_____

_____

_____

_____

_____

_____

_____

_____

_____

_____

_____

_____

_____

_____

_____

_____

_____

_____

_____

## LONELY THOUGHTS

# Lonely Thoughts

---

---

---

---

---

---

---

---

---

---

---

---

---

---

---

---

---

---

LONELY THOUGHTS

_____

_____

_____

_____

_____

_____

_____

_____

_____

_____

_____

_____

_____

_____

_____

_____

_____

_____

_____

_____

_____

_____

_____

_____

_____

_____

_____

_____

_____

_____

_____

_____

_____

_____

_____

_____

_____

_____

_____

_____

_____

_____

_____

_____

_____

_____

_____

_____

_____

_____

_____

_____

_____

_____

_____

_____

_____

_____

_____

_____

_____

# LONELY THOUGHTS

_____

_____

_____

_____

_____

_____

_____

_____

_____

_____

_____

_____

_____

_____

_____

_____

_____

_____

_____

_____

_____

_____

Dr. Kellye Bolar

Beautiful soul,

Now that you have taken the time to read my lonely thoughts and write some of your own, I would love to hear from you.  Share your thoughts with me by sending an email to _**kbeducationllc@gmail.com.**_  Let me know the good, the bad, the heartache, the pain, or anything else you would like to share.  I look forward to hearing from you and reading your lonely thoughts.

With love,

Dr. KB

Dr. Kellye Bolar

# ABOUT THE AUTHOR

Dr. Kellye Bolar is an education specialist, dance choreographer, poet, writer, speaker, coach, and youth mentor. She is passionate about educating the youth, creating dance choreography, family, love, adventure, and growth. Dr. Kellye Bolar was born and raised in Picayune, MS, and she currently resides in Ocean Springs, MS.

51321819R00100

Made in the USA
Columbia, SC
20 February 2019